Dialogue

For Lovers

SONNETS OF SHAKESPEARE
FOR DRAMATIC PRESENTATION

By Eve Merriam

SAMUEL FRENCH, INC.

25 WEST 45TH STREET   NEW YORK 10036
7623 SUNSET BOULEVARD   HOLLYWOOD 90046
LONDON   *TORONTO*

DIALOGUE FOR LOVERS was first presented at the Symphony Space, N.Y.C. on April 23, 1980 and was directed by Isaiah Sheffer. The set and costume designs were by Daniel Michaelson. The lighting was designed by Albert Bergeret. The Production stage manager was Gary Stein. The cast was as follows:

WOMAN .... Estelle Parsons
MAN .... Fritz Weaver
SOPRANO .... Sheila Schonbrun
MUSICIANS:
VIOLA DA GAMBA ..... Wendy Gillespie, Mary Springfels
LUTE PLAYER .... Jerry Willard

Lyrics and Music titles will be found following the text.

Dialogue For Lovers

*As house lights dim, musical introduction begins on Lute &
Viola. After a minute the* WOMAN *enters from stage left
and moves down stage center. After another minute the*
MAN *enters from stage left and crosses down stage.*
When MAN *notices* WOMAN, *music stops & love chord
is struck.*

Music
Cue #1

Music
Cue #2

WOMAN.
Cupid laid by his brand and fell asleep;
A maid of Dian's this advantage found,
    (*The* MAN *starts up and listens attentively.*)
And his love-kindling fire did quickly steep
In a cold valley-fountain of that ground;
Which borrowed from this holy fire of Love
A dateless lively heat, still to endure,
And grew a seething bath, which yet men prove
Against strange maladies a sovereign cure.
    MAN.
But at my mistress' eye Love's brand new-fired,
The boy for trial needs would touch my breast;
I, sick withal, the help of bath desired,
And thither hied, a sad distemper'd guest,
But found no cure: the bath for my help lies
Where Cupid got new fire, my mistress' eyes.
    WOMAN.
The little Love-god lying once asleep
Laid by his side his heart-inflaming brand,
Whilst many nymphs that vow'd chaste life to keep
Came tripping by;
    MAN. (*Interrupting her.*)
But in her maiden hand

5

The fairest votary took up that fire
Which many legions of true hearts had warm'd;
And so the general of hot desire
Was sleeping by a virgin hand disarm'd.
> WOMAN.

This brand she quenched in a cool well by,
Which from Love's fire took heat perpetual,
Growing a bath and healthful remedy
For men diseased;
> MAN.

>   but I, my mistress' thrall,
Came there for cure, and this by that I prove,
Love's fire heats water,
> WOMAN.

>   water cools not love.

Music
Cue #3
(They salute each other as the MUSIC, sprightly and fanciful, interweaves the two leitmotifs together. Light switches to pinkish tone.)

PART ONE: *Overtures to Love*

> WOMAN.

Love is too young to know what conscience is;
Yet who knows not conscience is born of love?
Then, gentle cheater, urge not my amiss,
Lest guilty of my faults thy sweet self prove:
For, thou betraying me, I do betray
My nobler part to my gross body's treason;
My soul doth tell my body that he may
Triumph in love;
> MAN.

>   flesh stays no farther reason,

But rising at thy name doth point out thee
As his triumphant prize. Proud of this pride,
He is contented thy poor drudge to be,
To stand in thy affairs, fall by thy side.
    No want of conscience hold it that I call
    Her 'love' for whose dear love I rise and fall.
My mistress' eyes are nothing like the sun;
Coral is far more red than her lips' red:
If snow be white, why then her breasts are dun;
If hairs be wires, black wires grow on her head.
I have seen roses damask'd, red and white,
But no such roses see I in her cheeks;
And in some perfumes is there more delight
Than in the breath that from my mistress reeks.
I love to hear her speak; yet well I know
That music hath a far more pleasing sound:
I grant I never saw a goddess go,
My mistress, when she walks, treads on the ground:
    And yet, by heaven, I think my love as rare
    As any she belied with false compare.
  WOMAN.
Against that time, if ever that time come,
When I shall see thee frown on my defects,
When as thy love hath cast his utmost sum,
Call'd to that audit by advised respects;
Against that time when thou shalt strangely pass,
And scarcely greet me with that sum, thine eye,
When love, converted from the thing it was,
Shall reasons find of settled gravity;
Against that time do I ensconce me here
Within the knowledge of mine own desert,
And this my hand against myself uprear,
To guard the lawful reasons on thy part:
    To leave poor me thou hast the strength of laws,
    Since why to love I can allege no cause.

MAN.

From fairest creatures we desire increase,
That thereby beauty's rose might never die,
But as the riper should by time decease,
His tender heir might bear his memory:
But thou, contracted to thine own bright eyes,
Feed'st thy light's flame with self-substantial fuel,
Making a famine where abundance lies,
Thyself thy foe, to they sweet self too cruel.
Thou that art now the world's fresh ornament
And only herald to the gaudy spring,
Within thine own bud buriest thy content
And, tender churl, makest waste in niggarding.
    Pity the world, or else this glutton be,
      To eat the world's due, by the grave and thee.

WOMAN. (*To her looking glass.*)

When forty winters shall besiege thy brow
And dig deep trenches in thy beauty's field,
Thy youth's proud livery, so gazed on now,
Will be a tatter'd weed, of small worth held:

MAN. (*Over her shoulder.*)

Then being ask'd where all thy beauty lies,
Where all the treasure of thy lusty days,
To say, within thine own deep-sunken eyes,
Were an all-eating shame and thriftless praise.
How much more praise deserved thy beauty's use,
If thou couldst answer 'This fair child of mine
Shall sum my count and make my old excuse,'
Proving his beauty by succession thine!
    This were to be new made when thou art old,
    And see thy blood warm when thou feel'st it cold.

(*She turns aside from him to busy herself with her costume,
    makeup, and then picks up a lute with bright ribbons
    on it. She smooths out the ribbons, tunes the instru-
    ment. Rejected, he starts to walk away.*)

MAN.

Farewell! thou art too dear for my possessing,
And like enough thou know'st thy estimate:
The charter of thy worth gives thee releasing;
My bonds in thee are all determinate.
For how do I hold thee but by thy granting?
And for that riches where is my deserving?
The cause of this fair gift in me is wanting,
And so my patent back again is swerving.
Thyself thou gavest, thy own worth then not knowing,
Or me, to whom thou gavest it, else mistaking;
So thy great gift, upon misprision growing,
Comes home again, on better judgement making.
  Thus have I had thee, as a dream doth flatter,
  In sleep a king, but waking no such matter.

(*She calls him back by SOUNDING a few chords on her
  lute.*)

WOMAN.

Music to hear, why hear'st thou music sadly?
  MAN.

Sweets with sweets war not, joy delights in joy.
Why lovest thou that which thou receivest not gladly,
Or else receivest with pleasure thine annoy?
  WOMAN.

If the true concord of well tuned sounds,
By unions married, do offend thine ear,
  MAN.

They do but sweetly chide thee, who confounds
In singleness the parts that thou shouldst bear.
  WOMAN. (*Deliberately provocative.*)

Mark how one string, sweet husband to another,
Strikes each in each by mutual ordering;
Resembling sire and child and happy mother,
Who, all in one, one pleasing note do sing:

MAN. (*Topping her.*)
Whose speechless song, being many, seeming one,
Sings this to thee: 'Thou single wilt prove none.'

Music
Cue #4

(*He embraces her; the lute slips from her fingers; lights
dim and Offstage MUSIC Picks up the lute song. The
MUSIC rises to a joyous climax and fades under, as
the lights come on again showing the lover with his
lass a-lap.*)

PART TWO: *Of Clinging Hearts and Lingering Departings*

MAN. (*As the conquering hero.*)
Shall I compare thee to a summer's day?
Thou art more lovely and more temperate:
Rough winds do shake the darling buds of May,
And summer's lease hath all too short a date:
Sometime too hot the eye of heaven shines,
And often is his gold complexion dimm'd;
And every fair from fair sometime declines,
By chance or nature's changing course untrimm'd;
But thy eternal summer shall not fade,
Nor lose possession of that fair thou owest;
Nor shall Death brag thou wander'st in his shade,
When in eternal lines to time thou grow'st:
     So long as men can breathe, or eyes can see,
     So long lives this, and this gives life to thee.
WOMAN. (*Stretching sleepily in the luxury of love.*)
Full many a glorious morning have I seen
Flatter the mountain-tops with sovereign eye,
Kissing with golden face the meadows green,
Gilding pale streams with heavenly alchemy;

Anon permit the basest clouds to ride
With ugly rack on his celestial face,
And from the forlorn world his visage hide,
Stealing unseen to west with this disgrace:
Even so my sun one early morn did shine
With all-triumphant splendour on my brow;
   (*She springs wakefully to reality.*)
But, out, alack! he was but one hour mine,
The region cloud hath mask'd him from me now.
      Yet him for this my love no whit disdaineth;
      Suns of the world may stain when heaven's sun
         staineth.
Let me confess that we two must be twain,
Although our undivided loves are one:
  MAN.
So shall those blots that do with me remain,
Without thy help, by me be borne alone.
  WOMAN.
In our two loves there is but one respect,
Though in our lives a separable spite,
Which though it alter not love's sole effect,
Yet doth it steal sweet hours from love's delight.
  MAN.
I may not evermore acknowledge thee
Lest my bewailed guilt should do thee shame,
Nor thou with public kindness honour me,
Unless thou take that honour from thy name:
  BOTH.
But do not so; I love thee in such sort
As thou being mine, mine is thy good report.
  MAN.
As a decrepit father takes delight
To see his active child do deeds of youth,
So I, made lame by fortune's dearest spite,
Take all my comfort of thy worth and truth;

For whether beauty, birth, or wealth, or wit,
Or any of these all, or all, or more,
Entitled in thy parts do crowned sit,
I make my love engrafted to this store:
So then I am not lame, poor, nor despised,
Whilst that this shadow doth such substance give
That I in thy abundance am sufficed
And by a part of all thy glory live.
    Look, what is best, that best I wish in thee:
    This wish I have; then ten times happy me!
  WOMAN.
O, how thy worth with manners may I sing,
When thou art all the better part of me?
What can mine own praise to mine own self bring?
And what is't but mine own when I praise thee?
Even for this let us divided live,
And our dear love lose name of single one,
That by this separation I may give
That due to thee which thou deservest alone.
O absence, what a torment wouldst thou prove,
Were it not thy sour leisure gave sweet leave
To entertain the time with thoughts of love,
Which time and thoughts so sweetly doth deceive,
    And that thou teachest how to make one twain,
    By praising him here who doth hence remain!

Music (*MUSIC denotes journeying apart. SOUND of carriage*
Cue #5   *wheels and horses.*)

  WOMAN.
How heavy do I journey on the way,
When what I seek, my weary travel's end,
Doth teach that ease and that repose to say,
'Thus far the miles are measured from thy friend!'
The beast that bears me, tired with my woe,

Plods dully on, to bear that weight in me,
As if by some instinct the wretch did know
His rider loved not speed, being made from thee:
The bloody spur cannot provoke him on
That sometimes anger thrusts into his hide;
Which heavily he answers with a groan,
More sharp to me than spurring to his side;
    For that same groan doth put this in my mind;
    My grief lies onward, and my joy behind.
  MAN.

Thus can my love excuse the slow offence
Of my dull bearer when from thee I speed:
From where thou art why should I haste me thence:
Till I return, of posting is no need.
O, what excuse will my poor beast then find,
When swift extremity can seem but slow?
Then should I spur, though mounted on the wind,
In winged speed no motion shall I know:
Then can no horse with my desire keep pace;
Therefore desire, of perfect'st love being made,
Shall neigh—no dull flesh—in his fiery race;
But love, for love, thus shall excuse my jade;
    Since from thee going he went willful-slow,
    Towards thee I'll run and give him leave to go.
  WOMAN.

Since I left you mine eye is in my mind,
And that which governs me to go about
Doth part his function and is partly blind,
Seems seeing, but effectually is out;
For it no form delivers to the heart
Of bird, of flower, or shape, which it doth latch:
Of his quick objects hath the mind no part,
Nor his own vision holds what it doth catch;
For if it see the rudest or gentlest sight,
The most sweet favour or deformed'st creature,

The mountain or the sea, the day or night,
The crow or dove, it shapes them to your feature:
    Incapable of more, replete with you,
     My most true mind thus maketh mine untrue.
  MAN.

Weary with toil, I haste me to my bed,
The dear repose for limbs with travel tired;
But then begins a journey in my head
To work my mind, when body's work's expired:
For then my thoughts, from far where I abide,
Intend a zealous pilgrimage to thee,
And keep my drooping eyelids open wide,
Looking on darkness which the blind do see:
Save that my soul's imaginary sight
Presents thy shadow to my sightless view,
Which, like a jewel hung in ghastly night,
Makes black night beauteous and her old face new.
    Lo, thus, by day my limbs, by night my mind,
     For thee and for myself no quiet find.
  WOMAN.

How can I then return in happy plight,
That am debarr'd the benefit of rest?
When day's oppression is not eased by night,
But day by night, and night by day, oppress'd?
And each, though enemies to either's reign,
Do in consent shake hands to torture me;
The one by toil, the other to complain
How far I toil, still farther off from thee.
I tell the day, to please him thou art bright,
And dost him grace when clouds do blot the heaven:
So flatter I the swart-complexion'd night;
When sparkling stars twire not thou gild'st the even.
    But day doth daily draw my sorrows longer,
     And night doth nightly make grief's strength
     seem stronger.

(MUSIC: elongated and sad, becomes stronger, takes on a   Music
durable melodic and measured beat.)   Cue #6

MAN.
Sweet love, renew thy force; be it not said
Thy edge should blunter be than appetite,
Which but to-day by feeding is allay'd,
To-morrow sharpen'd in his former might:
So, love, be thou; although to-day thou fill
Thy hungry eyes even till they wink with fullness,
To-morrow see again, and do not kill
The spirit of love with a perpetual dullness.
WOMAN.
Let this sad interim like the ocean be
Which parts the shore, where two contracted new
Come daily to the banks, that, when they see
Return of love, more blest may be the view;
BOTH.
Or call it winter, which, being full of care,
Makes summer's welcome thrice more wish'd, more rare.
MAN.
When, in disgrace with fortune and men's eyes,
I all alone beweep my outcast state,
And trouble deaf heaven with my bootless cries,
And look upon myself, and curse my fate,
Wishing me like to one more rich in hope,
Featured like him, like him with friends possess'd,
Desiring this man's art and that man's scope,
With what I most enjoy contented least;
Yet in these thoughts myself almost despising,
Haply I think on thee, and then my state,
Like to the lark at bread of day arising
From sullen earth, sings hymns at heaven's gate;
    For thy sweet love remember'd such wealth brings
    That then I scorn to change my state with kings.

WOMAN.

When to the sessions of sweet silent thought
I summon up remembrance of things past,
I sigh the lack of many a thing I sought,
And with old woes new wail my dear time's waste:
Then can I drown an eye, unused to flow,
For precious friends hid in death's dateless night,
And weep afresh love's long since cancell'd woe,
And moan the expense of many a vanish'd sight:
Then can I grieve at grievances foregone,
And heavily from woe to woe tell o'er
The sad account of fore-bemoaned moan,
Which I new pay as if not paid before.
  But if the while I think on thee, dear friend,
  All losses are restored and sorrows end.

MAN.

So am I as the rich, whose blessed key
Can bring him to his sweet up-locked treasure,
The which he will not every hour survey,
For blunting the fine point of seldom pleasure.

WOMAN.

Therefore are feasts so solemn and so rare,
Since, seldom coming, in the long year set,
Like stones of worth they thinly placed are,
Or captain jewels in the carcanet.
So is the time that keeps you as my chest,

MAN.

Or as the wardrobe which the robe doth hide,
To make some special instant special blest,
By new unfolding his imprison'd pride.

WOMAN.

Blessed are you, whose worthiness gives scope,

MAN.

Being had, to triumph, being lack'd, to hope.

Music
Cue #7

(*MUSIC: A swift birdlike passage, suggesting a brief
rendezvous and then separation again.*)

WOMAN.

How like a winter hath my absence been
From thee, the pleasure of the fleeting year:
What freezings have I felt, what dark days seen!
What old December's bareness every where!
And yet this time removed was summer's time;
The teeming autumn, big with rich increase,
Bearing the wanton burthen of the prime,
Like widowed wombs after their lords' decease:
Yet this abundant issue seem'd to me
But hope of orphans and unfather'd fruit;
For summer and his pleasure wait on thee,
And, thou away, the very birds are mute;
 Or, if they sing, 'tis with so dull a cheer
 That leaves look pale, dreading the winter's near.

MAN.

From you have I been absent in the spring,
When proud-pied April, dress'd in all his trim,
Hath put a spirit of youth in every thing,
That heavy Saturn laugh'd and leap'd with him.
Yet nor the lays of birds, nor the sweet smell
Of different flowers in odour and in hue,
Could make me any summer's story tell,
Or from their proud lap pluck them where they grew:
Nor did I wonder at the lily's white,
Nor praise the deep vermilion in the rose;
They were but sweet, but figures of delight,
Drawn after you, you pattern of all those.
 Yet seem'd it winter still, and, you away,
 As with your shadow I with these did play.

Music
Cue #8

(*LIGHTS DIM and MUSIC indicating jealousy begins to*

creep in and low-mutters under the following as the lights come on again, but in a purpled key after the saffron sunshine of earlier scenes.)

PART THREE: *Regions of Jealousy*

MAN.

Being your slave, what should I do but tend
Upon the hours and times of your desire?
I have no precious time at all to spend,
Nor services to do, till you require.
Nor dare I chide the world-without-end hour
Whilst I, my sovereign, watch the clock for you,
Nor think the bitterness of absence sour
When you have bid your servant once adieu;
Nor dare I question with my jealous thought
Where you may be, or your affairs suppose,
But, like a sad slave, stay and think of nought
Save, where you are how happy you make those.
    So true a fool is love that in your will,
    Though you do any thing, he thinks no ill.

WOMAN.

That god forbid that made me first your slave,
I should in thought control your times of pleasure,
Or at your hand the account of hours to crave,
Being your vassal, bound to stay your leisure!

MAN.

O, let me suffer, being at your beck,
The imprison'd absence of your liberty;
And patience, tame to sufferance, bide each check,
Without accusing you of injury.

WOMAN.

Be where you list, your charter is so strong
That you yourself may privilege your time
To what you will; to you it doth belong
Yourself to pardon of self-doing crime.

MAN.

I am to wait, though waiting so be hell,
Not blame your pleasure, be it ill or well.
But do thy worst to steal thyself away,
For term of life thou art assured mine;

    WOMAN.

And life no longer than thy love will stay,
For it depends upon that love of thine.

    MAN.

Then need I not to fear the worst of wrongs,
When in the least of them my life hath end.

    WOMAN.

I see a better state to me belongs
Than that which on thy humour doth depend:

    MAN.

Thou canst not vex me with inconstant mind,
Since that my life on thy revolt doth lie.
O, what a happy title do I find,
Happy to have thy love, happy to die!

    WOMAN.

But what's so blessed-fair that fears no blot?
Thou mayst be false, and yet I know it not.

(*The MUSIC begins to agitate her too; tones of jealous
discord flare up and bubble down under again.*)

    WOMAN.

Some glory in their birth, some in their skill,
Some in their wealth, some in their body's force;
Some in their garments, though new-fangled ill;
Some in their hawks and hounds, some in their horse;
And every humour hath his adjunct pleasure,
Wherein it finds a joy above the rest:
But these particulars are not my measure;
All these I better in one general best.
Thy love is better than high birth to me,

Richer than wealth, prouder than garments' cost,
Of more delight than hawks or horses be;
And having thee, of all men's pride I boast:
> Wretched in this alone, that thou mayst take
> All this away and me most wretched make.

MAN.

So shall I live, supposing thou art true,
Like a deceived husband; so love's face
May still seem love to me, though alter'd new;
Thy looks with me, thy heart in other place:
For there can live no hatred in thine eye,
Therefore in that I cannot know thy change.
In many's looks the false heart's history
Is writ in moods and frowns and wrinkles strange,
But heaven in thy creation did decree
That in thy face sweet love should ever dwell;
Whate'er thy thoughts or thy heart's workings be,
Thy looks should nothing thence but sweetness tell.
> How like Eve's apple doth thy beauty grow,
> If thy sweet virtue answer not thy show!

Then hate me when thou wilt; if ever, now;
Now, while the world is bent my deeds to cross,
Join with the spite of fortune, make me bow,
And do not drop in for an after-loss:
Ah, do not, when my heart hath 'scaped this sorrow,
Come in the rearward of a conquer'd woe;
Give not a windy night a rainy morrow,
To linger out a purposed overthrow.
If thou wilt leave me, do not leave me last,
When other petty griefs have done their spite,
But in the onset come: so shall I taste
At first the very worst of fortune's might;
> And other strains of woe, which now seem woe,
> Compared with loss of thee will not seem so.

WOMAN.

Those pretty wrongs that liberty commits,

When I am sometime absent from thy heart,
Thy beauty and thy years full well befits,
For still temptation follows where thou art.
Gentle thou art, and therefore to be won,
Beauteous thou art, therefore to be assailed;
And when a woman woos, what woman's son
Will sourly leave her till she have prevailed?
Ay me! but yet thou mightst my seat forbear,
And chide thy beauty and thy straying youth,
Who lead thee in their riot even there
Where thou art forced to break a twofold truth,
    Hers, by thy beauty tempting her to thee,
    Thine, by thy beauty being false to me.
In loving thee thou know'st I am forsworn,
But thou art twice forsworn to me love swearing;
In act thy bed-vow broke, and new faith torn,
In vowing new hate after new love bearing.
But why of two oaths' breach do I accuse thee,
When I break twenty? I am perjured most;
For all my vows are oaths but to misuse thee,
And all my honest faith in thee is lost:
For I have sworn deep oaths of thy deep kindness,
Oaths of thy love, thy truth, thy constancy;
And, to enlighten thee, gave eyes to blindness,
Or made them swear against the thing they see;
    For I have sworn thee fair; more perjured I,
    To swear against the truth so foul a lie!
    MAN. (*Trying to make her understand—he is only put-
ting his foot deeper into his mouth.*)
Thy bosom is endeared with all hearts
Which I by lacking have supposed dead;
And there reigns love, and all love's loving parts,
And all those friends which I thought buried.
How many a holy and obsequious tear
Hath dear religious love stol'n from mine eye,
As interest of the dead, which now appear

But things removed that hidden in thee lie!
Thou art the grave where buried love doth live,
Hung with the trophies of my lovers gone,
Who all their parts of me to thee did give;
That due of many now is thine alone:
    Their images I loved I view in thee,
      And thou, all they, hast all the all of me.

WOMAN. (*Making the most of scornfulness, since she imagines herself the "Hell-hath-no-fury-like—".*)
They that have power to hurt and will do none,
That do not do the thing they most do show,
Who, moving others, are themselves as stone,
Unmoved, cold and to temptation slow;
They rightly do inherit heaven's graces
And husband nature's riches from expense;
They are the lords and owners of their faces,
Others but stewards of their excellence.
The summer's flower is to the summer sweet,
Though to itself it only live and die,
But if that flower with base infection meet,
The basest weed outbraves his dignity:
    For sweetest things turn sourest by their deeds;
    Lilies that fester smell far worse than weeds.

MAN. (*Returning sarcasm in un-kind.*)
Some say, thy fault is youth, some wantonness;
Some say, thy grace is youth and gentle sport;
Both grace and faults are loved of more and less:
Thou makest faults graces that to thee resort.
As on the finger of a throned queen
The basest jewel will be well esteem'd,
So are those errors that in thee are seen
To truths translated and for true things deem'd.
How many lambs might the stern wolf betray,
If like a lamb he could his looks translate!
How many gazers mightst thou lead away,
If thou wouldst use the strength of all thy state!

But do not so; I love thee in such sort,
    As thou being mine, mine is thy good report.
    (*Calling upon philosophy and heaven since earthbound
    woman is so uncomprehending of his spirit—.*)
The expense of spirit in a waste of shame
Is lust in action; and till action, lust
Is perjured, murderous, bloody, full of blame,
Savage, extreme, rude, cruel, not to trust;
Enjoy'd no sooner but despised straight;
Past reason hunted; and no sooner had,
Past reason hated, as a swallowed bait,
On purpose laid to make the taker mad:
Mad in pursuit, and in possession so;
Had, having, and in quest to have, extreme;
A bliss in proof, and proved, a very woe;
Before, a joy proposed; behind a dream.
        All this the world well knows; yet none knows well
        To shun the heaven that leads men to this hell.
    WOMAN. (*Come back to earth you—.*)
Thou art as tyrannous, so as thou art,
As those whose beauties proudly make them cruel;
For well thou know'st to my dear doting heart
Thou art the fairest and most precious jewel.
Yet, in good faith, some say that thee behold,
Thy face hath not the power to make love groan:
To say they err I dare not be so bold,
Although I swear it to myself alone.
And to be sure that is not false I swear,
A thousand groans, but thinking on thy face,
One on another's neck, do witness bear
Thy black is fairest in my judgement's place.
        In nothing art thou black save in thy deeds,
        And thence this slander, as I think, proceeds.

(*MUSIC stabs the point home—a love motif tries to insinu-* Music
    ate into the jealousy.)   Cue #9

WOMAN.

My love is as a fever, longing still
For that which longer nurseth the disease;
Feeding on that which doth preserve the ill,
The uncertain sickly appetite to please.

MAN.

My reason, the physician to my love,
Angry that his prescriptions are not kept,
Hath left me, and I desperate now approve
Desire is death, which physic did except.
Past cure I am, now reason is past care,
And frantic-mad with evermore unrest;

WOMAN.

My thoughts and my discourse as madmen's are,
At random from the truth vainly express'd;
    For I have sworn thee fair, and thought thee bright,
    Who art as black as hell, as dark as night.

MAN.

Alas, 'tis true I have gone here and there,
And made myself a motley to the view,
Gored mine own thoughts, sold cheap what is most dear,
Made old offences of affections new;
Most true it is that I have look'd on truth
Askance and strangely: but, by all above,
These blenches gave my heart another youth,
And worse essays proved thee my best of love.
Now all is done, have what shall have no end:
Mine appetite I never more will grind
On newer proof, to try an old friend,
A god in love, to whom I am confined.
    Then give me welcome, next my heaven the best,
    Even to thy pure and most most loving breast.
*(And—as if the above alibi-ing conceit were not enough
—he goes on explaining.)*
Accuse me thus: that I have scanted all
Wherein I should your great deserts repay,

Forgot upon your dearest love to call,
Whereto all bonds do tie me day by day;
That I have frequent been with unknown minds,
And given to time your own dear-purchased right;
That I have hoisted sail to all the winds
Which should transport me farthest from your sight.
Book both my wilfulness and errors down,
And on just proof surmiss accumulate;
Bring me within the level of your frown,
But shoot not at me in your waken'd hate;
    Since my appeal says I did strive to prove
    The constancy and virtue of your love.

  WOMAN. (*Mimicking his own earlier words to her.*)
"My mistress' eyes are nothing like the sun;
Coral is far more red than her lips' red:
If snow be white, why then her breasts are dun;
If hairs be wires, black wires grow on her head.
I have seen roses damask'd, red and white,
But no such roses see I in her cheeks;
And in some perfumes is there more delight
Than in the breath that from my mistress reeks.
I love to hear her speak; yet well I know
That music hath a far more pleasing sound:
I grant I never saw a goddess go,
My mistress, when she walks, treads on the ground:
    And yet, by heaven, I think my love as rare
    As any she belied with false compare."

  MAN. (*Angered in earnest—who steals my verse steals passion.*)
How sweet and lovely dost thou make the shame
Which, like a canker in the fragrant rose,
Doth spot the beauty of thy budding name!
O, in what sweets dost thou thy sins inclose!
That tongue that tells the story of thy days,
Making lascivious comments on thy sport,
Cannot dispraise but in a kind of praise;

Naming thy name blesses an ill report.
O, what a mansion have those vices got
Which for their habitation chose out thee,
Where beauty's veil doth cover every blot
And all things turn to fair that eyes can see!
      Take heed, dear heart, of this large privilege;
      The hardest knife ill used doth lose his edge.

   WOMAN. (*Proceeding on the all-men-are-alike theory
and recognizing the necessity of loving this particular
male.*)

Thou blind fool, Love, what dost thou to mine eyes,
That they behold, and see not what they see?
They know what beauty is, see where it lies,
Yet what the best is take the worst to be.
If eyes, corrupt by over-partial looks,
Be anchor'd in the bay where all men ride,
Why of eyes' falsehood hast thou forged hooks,
Whereto the judgement of my heart is tied?
Why should my heart think that a several plot
Which my heart knows the wide world's common place?
Or mine eyes seeing this, say this is not,
To put fair truth upon so foul a face?
      In things right true my heart and eyes have erred,
      And to this false plague are they now transferred.

   MAN. (*Picking up a bit of realism too.*)

In faith, I do not love thee with mine eyes,
For they in thee a thousand errors note;
But 'tis my heart that loves what they despise,
Who, in despite of view, is pleased to dote;
Nor are mine ears with thy tongue's tune delighted;
Nor tender feeling, to base touches prone,
Nor taste, nor smell, desire to be invited
To any sensual feast with thee alone:
But my five wits nor my five senses can
Dissuade one foolish heart from serving thee;
Who leaves unsway'd the likeness of a man,

Thy proud heart's slave and vassal wretch to be:
    Only my plague thus far I count my gain,
    That she that makes me sin awards me pain.
  WOMAN.

Be wise as thou art cruel; do not press
My tongue-tied patience with too much disdain;
Lest sorrow lend me words, and words express
The manner of my pity-wanting pain.
  MAN.

If I might teach thee wit, better it were,
Though not to love, yet, love, to tell me so;
As testy sick men, when their deaths be near,
No news but health from their physicians know;
For, if I should despair, I should grow mad,
And in my madness might speak ill of thee:
Now this ill-wresting world is grown so bad,
Mad slanderers by mad ears believed be.
  BOTH.

That I may not be so, nor thou belied,
Bear thine eyes straight, though thy proud heart go wide.

(*MUSIC: their two leitmotifs mingle for a moment, then* Music
    separate again.) Cue #10

  WOMAN. (*The fault is mine.*)
Two loves I have of comfort and despair,
Which like two spirits do suggest me still:
The better angel is a man right fair,
The worser spirit a woman colour'd ill.
To win me soon to hell, my female evil
Tempteth my better angel from my side,
And would corrupt my saint to be a devil,
Wooing his purity with her foul pride.
And whether that my angel be turn'd fiend
Suspect I may, yet not directly tell;

But being both from me, both to each friend,
I guess one angel in another's hell:
> Yet this shall I ne'er know, but live in doubt,
> Till my bad angel fire my good one out.

MAN. (*No, dear love, the fault is mine.*)
Say that thou didst forsake me for some fault,
And I will comment upon that offense:
Speak of my lameness, and I straight will halt,
Against thy reasons making no defense.
Thou canst not, love, disgrace me half so ill,
To set a form upon desired change,
As I'll myself disgrace; knowing thy will,
I will acquaintance strangle and look strange;
Be absent from thy walks; and in my tongue
Thy sweet beloved name no more shall dwell,
Lest I, too much profane, should do it wrong,
And haply of our old acquaintance tell.
> For thee, against myself I'll vow debate,
> For I must ne'er love him whom thou dost hate.

WOMAN.
That you were once unkind befriends me now,
And for that sorrow which I then did feel
Needs must I under my transgression bow,
Unless my nerves were brass or hammer'd steel.

MAN.
For if you were by my unkindness shaken,
As I by yours, you've pass'd a hell of time;
And I, a tyrant, have no leisure taken
To weigh how once I suffer'd in your crime.

WOMAN.
O, that our night of woe might have remember'd
My deepest sense, how hard true sorrow hits,
And soon to you, as you tó me, then tender'd
The humble salve which wounded bosoms fits!

MAN.
But that your trespass now becomes a fee;
Mine ransoms yours, and yours must ransom me.

(The MUSIC of happy reconciliation starts up and under-
scores the following.)

MAN.

O, never say that I was false of heart,
Though absence seem'd my flame to qualify.
As easy might I from myself depart
As from my soul, which in thy breast doth lie:
That is my home of love: if I have ranged,
Like him that travels, I return again;

WOMAN.

Just to the time, not with the time exchanged,
So that myself bring water for my stain.
Never believe, though in my nature reign'd
All frailties that besiege all kinds of blood,
That it could so preposterously be stain'd,
To leave for nothing all thy sum of good;

BOTH.

For nothing this wide universe I call,
Save thou, my rose; in it thou art my all.

(Lights bright and MUSIC full and rich.)   Music
                                                Cue #11

PART FOUR: *Of Time and Timeless Love*

(Lights change to copper autumnal tone; the MUSIC dulcet, Music
slower.)   Cue #12

WOMAN.

To me, fair friend, you never can be old,
For as you were when first your eye I eyed,
Such seems your beauty still. Three winters' cold
Have from the forests shook three summers' pride,
Three beauteous springs to yellow autumn turn'd
In process of the seasons have I seen,
Three April perfumes in three hot Junes burn'd,
Since first I saw you fresh, which yet are green.

Ah, yet doth beauty, like a dial-hand,
Steal from his figure, and no pace perceived;
So your sweet hue, which methinks still doth stand,
Hath motion, and mine eye may be deceived:
> For fear of which, hear this, thou age unbred;
> Ere you were born was beauty's summer dead.

MAN.

When my love swears that she is made of truth,
I do believe her, though I know she lies,
That she might think me some untutor'd youth,
Unlearned in the world's false subtleties.
Thus vainly thinking that she thinks me young,
Although she knows my days are past the best,
Simply I credit her false-speaking tongue:
On both sides thus is simple truth suppress'd
But wherefore says she not she is unjust?
And wherefore say not I that I am old?
O, love's best habit is in seeming trust,
And age in love loves not to have years told:
> Therefore I lie with her and she with me,
> And in our faults by lies we flatter'd be.

WOMAN. (*Gazes in her looking glass and puts it aside to gaze more fondly into her aging lover's eyes.*)

Sin of self-love possesseth all mine eye
And all my soul and all my every part;
And for this sin there is no remedy,
It is so grounded inward in my heart.
Methinks no face so gracious is as mine,
No shape so true, no truth of such account,
And for myself mine own worth do define,
As I all other in all worths surmount.
But when my glass shows me myself indeed.
Beated and chopp'd with tann'd antiquity,
Mine own self-love quite contrary I read;
Self so self-loving were iniquity.
> 'Tis thee, myself, that for myself I praise,
> Painting my age with beauty of thy days.

MAN.

When I have seen by Time's fell hand defaced
The rich-proud cost of outworn buried age;
When sometime lofty towers I see down-razed,
And brass eternal slave to mortal rage;

WOMAN.

When I have seen the hungry ocean gain
Advantage on the kingdom of the shore,
And the firm soil win of the watery main,
Increasing store with loss and loss with store:

MAN.

When I have seen such interchange of state,
Or state itself confounded to decay;

WOMAN.

Ruin hath taught me thus to ruminate,
That Time will come and take my lover away.
    This thought is as a death, which cannot choose
    But weep to have that which it fears to lose.

MAN.

Not mine own fears, nor the prophetic soul
Of the wide world dreaming on things to come,
Can yet the lease of my true love control,
Supposed as forfeit to a confined doom.
The mortal moon hath her eclipse endured,
And the sad augurs mock their own presage;
Incertainties now crown themselves assured,
And peace proclaims olives of endless age.
Now with the drops of this most balmy time
My love looks fresh, and Death to me subscribes,
Since, spite of him, I'll live in this poor rhyme,
While he insults o'er dull and speechless tribes:
    And thou in this shalt find thy monument,
    When tyrants' crests and tombs of brass are spent.

WOMAN.

When I consider every thing that grows
Holds in perfection but a little moment,
That this huge stage presenteth nought but shows

Whereon the stars in secret influence comment;
When I perceive that men as plants increase,
Cheered and check'd even by the self-same sky,
Vaunt in their youthful sap, at height decrease,
And wear their brave state out of memory;
Then the conceit of this inconstant stay
Sets you most rich in youth before my sight,
Where wasteful Time debateth with Decay,
To change your day of youth to sullied night;
  And all in war with Time for love of you,
  As he takes from you, I engraft you new.
 MAN.
Let me not to the marriage of true minds
Admit impediments. Love is not love
Which alters when it alteration finds,
Or bends with the remover to remove:
O, no! it is an ever-fixed mark,
That looks on tempests and is never shaken;
It is the star to every wandering bark,
Whose worth's unknown, although his height be taken.
Love's not Time's fool, though rosy lips and cheeks
Within his bending sickle's compass come;
Love alters not with his brief hours and weeks,
But bears it out even to the edge of doom.
  If this be error and upon me proved,
  I never writ, nor no man ever loved.

Music
Cue #13
   (*MUSIC for finale comes under the following.*)

 MAN.
Not marble, nor the gilded monuments
Of princes, shall outlive this powerful rhyme;
But you shall shine more bright in these contents
Than unswept stone, besmear'd with sluttish time.
 WOMAN.
When wasteful war shall statues overturn,

And broils root out the work of masonry,
Nor Mars his sword nor war's quick fire shall burn
The living record of your memory.

MAN.

'Gainst death and all-oblivious enmity
Shall you pace forth; your praise shall still find room
Even in the eyes of all posterity
That wear this world out to the ending doom.

BOTH.

So, till the judgement that yourself arise,
You live in this, and dwell in lovers' eyes.

Music
Cue #14

Music Used in "DIALOGUE FOR LOVERS"
as performed at
Symphony Space, New York City April 1980

MUSIC CUE # 1—A Fancy #5 by John Dowland
Lute
MUSIC CUE # 2—Spirit of Gambo by Tobias Hume
Viola da Gamba
MUSIC CUE # 3—Wolsey's Wilde by William Byrd
Lute and
Gamba (Treble)
MUSIC CUE # 4—Come Again by John Dowland
Voice and Lute
MUSIC CUE # 5—Now O Now I Needs Must Part by
John Dowland
Voice and Lute
MUSIC CUE # 6—Frog Galliard by John Dowland
Lute
MUSIC CUE # 7—Hark, Hark by Tobias Hume
Viola da Gamba
MUSIC CUE # 8—Can She Excuse by John Dowland
Voice and Lute
MUSIC CUE # 9—Fire, Fire by Thomas Campion
Voice and Lute
MUSIC CUE #10—Pavin #42 by Tobias Hume
Viola da Gamba
MUSIC CUE #11—See Mine Own Sweet Jewel by
Thomas Morley
Voice, Treble
Viol, Lute
MUSIC CUE #12—Flow My Tears by John Dowland
Lute
MUSIC CUE #13—Fortune My Foe by John Dowland
Lute

34

MUSIC CUE #14—Fine Knacks For Ladies by
                    John Dowland

                              Voice, Lute,
                              Bass Viol
                              da Gamba

MUSIC CUE#4

          ''Come Again Sweet Love Doth Now Invite''

Come again:
Sweet love doth now invite,
Thy graces that refrain,
To do me due delight,
To see, to hear, to touch, to kiss, to die,
With thee again in sweetest sympathy.
To see, to hear, to touch, to kiss, to die,
With thee again in sweetest sympathy.

All the day
The sun doth lends me shine.
By frowns do cause me pine,
And feeds me with delay,
Her smiles, her springs that makes my joys to grow.
Her frowns her frowns, the winters of my woe:
Her smiles, her springs that makes my joys to grow,
Her frowns her frowns, the winters of my woe.

Gentle love
Draw forth thy wounding dart,
Thou canst not pierce her heart,
For I that to approve
By sighs and tears more hot than are thy shafts,
Did tempt while she for triumph laughs.

By sighs and tears more hot than are thy shafts,
Did tempt while she for triumph laughs.

MUSIC CUE #5

"Now, O now, I Needs Must Part"

Now, O now, I needs must part,
Parting though I absent mourn.
Absence can no joy impart:
Joy once fled cannot return.
While I live I needs must love,
Loves lives not when Hope is gone.
Now at last despair doth prove,
Love divided loveth not.

Sad despair doth drive me hence,
This despair unkindness sends.
If that parting be offence,
It is she which then offends.

Sad despair doth drive me hence,
This despair unkindness sends.
If that parting be offence,
It is she which then offends.

MUSIC CUE #8

"Can She Excuse My Wrongs"

Was I so base that I might not aspire
Unto those high joys which she holds from me?
As they are high is my desire:
If she this deny, what only granted be?

If she will yield to that which reason is,
It is reason's will that love should be just.
Dear make me happy still by granting this,
Or cut off delays if that I die must.

Better a thousand times to die,
Than for a live thus still tormented:
Dear, but remember it was I
Who for thy sake did die contented.

Better a thousand times to die,
Than for a live thus still tormented:
Dear, but remember it was I
Who for thy sake did die contented.

MUSIC CUE #9

FIRE, FIRE

Fire, fire. Fire, fire. Lo here I burn,
I burn in such desire, That all the tears
that I can strain,
Out of mine I die empty brain,
Can not allay my scorching pain.
Come, Trent and Homber fair Thames.
Dread Ocean haste with all thy streams.
And if you can not quench my fire.
O drown both me. O drown both me and my desire.
O drown both me. O drown both me and my desire.

MUSIC CUE #11

"See, Mine Own Sweet Jewel"

Now, Now, mine own sweet flower,
Mine own sweet flower,
Mine own sweet flower,
What I have,
What I have,

What I have for my darling,
A garden, garden growing overflowing,
A garden growing roses showing
All in bloom through the year
For my dear,
Never say'st that I love not,
For I do love thee unfading,
My garden constant ever.

All in bloom through the year
For my dear,
Never say'st that I love not,
For I do love thee unfading,
My garden will never close.

MUSIC CUE #14

"Fine Knacks For Ladies"

Loo, Hallelooia,
Halleloo, Loo, Loo!
Two hearts are won,
A new life has begun.
Ladies and gentlemen,
Bid you adieu.
Where'er you may go,
Whate'er you may do:
Though all the world play false,
The heart is true,
The heart is true,
The heart is true.

Loo, Hallelooia,
Halleloo, Loo, Loo!
One heart from one,

Unhappy then is none.
Ladies and gentlemen,
Bid you adieu.
Where'er you may go,
Whate'er you may do:
Though all the world play false
The heart is true,
The heart is true,
The heart is true.

PROPERTY LIST

1 small hand mirror for woman
1 Lute pre set stage left—used by woman
1 Ring carried by woman, given as gift to man
1 Pendant with gem carried by man, given as gift to woman

COSTUME PLOT

The costumes are contemporary with a ''period'' look.

WOMAN
peachy-pink satin bias underdress
beige satin stripe chiffon undersleeves
beige gauze caftan
red neck ribbon
beige canvas slippers
cream hooded cape (for traveling)

MAN
''Romantic'' cream cotton nubby shirt
gray-blue velvet trousers
charcoal hopsack vest with black leather trim
black shoes and socks
gray wool cape (for traveling)

FEMALE SINGER (androgynous look)
peach ''Romantic'' crepe shirt
long black wool sleeveless vest
pinky-gray velvet pants
gray suede boots

FEMALE MUSICIAN
pinky-gray long crepe dress
pink sash and bow
gray slippers

MALE MUSICIAN
black raw silk shirt
gray cotton peasant overshirt
gray knit pants
black shoes and socks

41

BOOKS ON THE THEATRE

REFERENCE POINT

By Arthur Hopkins

Having brought to our stage new methods of production as simple as they were revolutionary, Mr. Hopkins in *Reference Point* recapitulates personal theories, practices and conclusions on stage direction and production. It is a theatre book based on a series of papers read by Arthur Hopkins at the 1947 Theatre Seminar at Fordham University for drama teachers, directors and students from all parts of the country. It is best termed a book of practical idealism, for it is concerned with creative ways in writing, acting, and directing, and access to their source. "I want to stand up and cheer . . . Mr. Hopkins combed his memories, reflected on his principles and came up with some mighty sound, helpful and even inspiring comment." —Harry Hansen, *N. Y. World-Telegram*.

MODERN ACTING: A MANUAL

By Sophie Rosenstein, Larrae A. Haydon, Wilbur Sparrow.

The fundamentals of acting as taught at the University of Washington are compressed clearly and usefully in these pages. The approach and method are described and illustrated so that others may adopt them and profit by them.

PROBLEM PROJECTS IN ACTING

By Katherine Kester

Here are thirty scenes, varying from two to twelve minutes, which are so arranged that each scene appears as a complete unit and not as an excerpt from a longer work. The problem-project method is to emphasize the one important problem in a scene, and at the same time to correlate all the other factors involved in acting.

THE ACTOR CREATES

By Aristide D'Angelo, M.A., LL.B., instructor at the American Academy of Dramatics Arts.

This book originally intended for the use of students at the American Academy of Dramatic Arts, is addressed to actors, directors, teachers, and to that larger audience interested in the appreciation of play presentation.